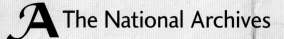
The National Archives

WORLD WAR I

UNCLASSIFIED

Secrets of World War I Revealed

NICK HUNTER

A & C BLACK
AN IMPRINT OF BLOOMSBURY
LONDON   NEW DELHI   NEW YORK   SYDNEY

Published 2014 by A & C Black,
an imprint of Bloomsbury Publishing Plc,
50 Bedford Square
London, WC1B 3DP

www.bloomsbury.com

Bloomsbury is a registered trademark of Bloomsbury Publishing Plc

Design by Nick Avery Design

ISBN: 978-1-4729-0525-3

A CIP catalogue for this book is available from the British Library.

Printed in China by Toppan Excel

1 3 5 7 9 10 8 6 4 2

CONTENTS

TERROR IN THE TRENCHES

At 07.30 a.m. on 1 July 1916, in the misty valley of the River Somme in northern France, the deafening artillery bombardment paused. Whistles signalled that the time had come. The first wave of 66,000 men left their trenches and marched steadily across no man's land. Some of the soldiers even kicked a football between them as they advanced. They were confident. Surely the enemy could not have survived nearly three million shells that had rained down on them for six days and six nights.

▲ As soon as the troops left their trenches, they were exposed to the full force of the enemy's weapons.

False hopes

As the infantry approached the German trenches, the real situation became clear. The artillery attack had not cleared the dense coils of barbed wire protecting the trenches. German machine guns that had remained underground during the terrible bombardment opened fire. The advancing troops had no protection from these deadly weapons. Dead and injured soldiers fell into the mud in their thousands.

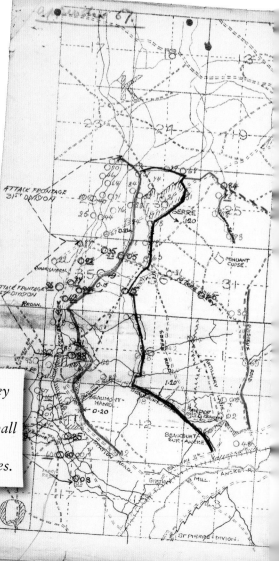

◀ Soldiers of the East Surrey Regiment, led by Captain Wilfred Nevill, played football as they moved steadily towards the German trenches.

This was the first day of the Battle of the Somme. In the following days the scale of the disaster became clear. Of 100,000 men who had advanced on that day, 20,000 had been killed and 40,000 injured. More British lives were lost in battle than on any day before or since.

The Battle of the Somme raged until November 1916 and claimed hundreds of thousands more lives on both sides. It has come to symbolize the horrors of World War I, but it was just one day of a conflict that changed the world forever. This book uses incredible archive material to discover the secrets of this terrible war, and to tell the story of those who fought it.

▲ *Millions of kilometres of razor-sharp barbed wire stopped attackers reaching the enemy trenches in World War I.*

◀ *This map shows the land, criss-crossed with trenches, that was fought over during the Battle of the Somme.*

A soldier's letter home about the first day of Somme

"The officers were urging us on... But you just couldn't. It was hopeless. And these young officers, going ahead... they were picked off like flies."

▲ *Nearly three million shells were fired at the German defences in the days before the advance of 1 July 1916.*

5

EUROPE DIVIDED

World War I lasted from the summer of 1914 until November 1918, but the story of World War I began long before the first shots were fired. It was an explosion of tensions and rivalries that had been building up in Europe for many decades.

Europe's most powerful nations, including France, Russia, and Great Britain, had long been rivals for influence in the world. In 1871, they were joined by a new and powerful nation: Germany. Prussia and a collection of smaller German states had united as a single country after a war against France in 1870-71.

▲ *The pink areas on this map show the size of the British Empire in the years before 1914.*

Taking sides

The new power in Europe worried other nations, but Germany did not feel secure. France wanted revenge after Germany had seized the states of Alsace and Lorraine. Germany's leaders were worried about being encircled by France and Russia. These Great Powers started making deals and alliances to protect themselves. By 1914, Europe was divided, with Germany, Austria-Hungary and Italy on one side, and the Triple Entente of Britain, France and Russia on the other.

▼ *Uniforms and weapons of war were very different in 1914 than they had been during the Franco-Prussian War.*

European nations had used their power to conquer other lands and build empires around the world. The largest of these was the British Empire, but France, Germany and others set up colonies in Africa and elsewhere. In southeastern Europe, the Turkish Ottoman Empire was falling apart as nations such as Serbia fought to become independent. Russia and Austria-Hungary were each trying to get more influence over the Balkan region and these new nations.

Talking tough

As the tension mounted, nations were desperate to show they were tougher than the rest. Germany and Britain competed to build the most powerful warships, called Dreadnoughts. In Britain, novels and newspapers warned that German spies were everywhere, planning for invasion. However, only ten suspected spies were actually arrested between 1911 and July 1914.

▶ *Many homing pigeons were shot to stop them passing messages to the enemy. This was strictly forbidden once war broke out as governments needed pigeons to pass secret messages.*

▲ *This is the death sentence passed on Carl Hans Lody, a German spy who used the name Charles Inglis. Lody was shot at the Tower of London on 6 November 1914.*

THE ROAD TO WAR

Fierce rivalries and edgy alliances meant there was a danger that a tiny dispute could spark a crisis that would quickly spiral out of control. Each country had war plans detailing how they would fight a war, but one plan in particular made a wider European war more likely.

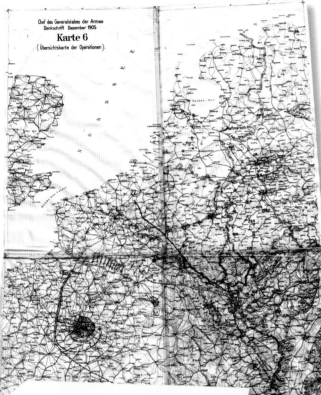

Chef des Generalstabes der Armee
Denkschrift Dezember 1905
Karte 6
(Übersichtskarte der Operationen).

▲ *This map shows the details of Germany's Schlieffen Plan, developed in 1905. It was only known to Germany's most senior military leaders.*

The Schlieffen Plan

Germany knew that they would probably have to fight against France and Russia, to the west and east. Their plan, called the Schlieffen Plan after the general who devised it, was to invade France through Belgium and deliver a knockout blow within a few weeks. Once France was defeated, they could turn their attention to the vast armies of Russia in the east. If this plan was put into action, Europe would be at war.

▲ *After shooting Archduke Franz Ferdinand and his wife, Gavrilo Princip was arrested. Investigators were able to link the plot to the Serbian government.*

Shot in Sarajevo

The first shot of World War I was fired in the Bosnian city of Sarajevo by a Serbian nationalist called Gavrilo Princip. Princip's assassination of the Archduke Franz Ferdinand, the heir to Austria-Hungary's throne, on 28 June 1914 was an outrage that Austria-Hungary could not ignore.

The shot set off a dramatic chain of events as Austria-Hungary blamed Serbia:

23 July: Austria-Hungary sends an ultimatum to Serbia making demands that they knew the Serbs would never accept.

28 July: After Serbia refuses to accept its demands, Austria-Hungary declares war on Serbia, with support from Germany.

30 July: Russia mobilises its huge army in support of Serbia.

1 August: Germany declares war on Russia. Germany's war plan means that its first attack will be against Russia's ally France through neutral Belgium.

3 August: Germany invades Belgium, Luxembourg and France.

4 August: Great Britain declares war on Germany because of its invasion of Belgium.

▼ *The Russian army could call on millions of men, but they lagged behind their opponents in the quality of their equipment and leadership.*

▲ *On 29 July, Tsar Nicholas II of Russia exchanged telegrams with his cousin Kaiser Wilhelm II of Germany in a desperate attempt to halt the slide to war. The Russian royal family would not live to see the end of the conflict.*

British Colonel **Alfred Knox** sent this dispatch detailing the mobilisation of Russian forces. He stated that preparations began on 24 August, the day after Austria-Hungary's ultimatum to Serbia.

"The number of men called up is causing general astonishment. Russians speak of an army of 8 million, but admit it will require 6 months to equip."

HOME BY CHRISTMAS?

The outbreak of war in August 1914 was greeted by enthusiastic crowds in cities across Europe. They cheered and sang patriotic songs. Many people believed that the war would be over by Christmas.

▲ *This Irish poster used the fear of German invasion to attract volunteers.*

Others, such as the British Minister for War Lord Kitchener, warned that the struggle would be long and bloody. Across Europe, astonishing numbers of men were sent off to fight in August 1914. In France, Germany and other European countries, most young men were expected to do military service. Germany could call on 4.3 million trained soldiers in 1914. More than 2000 trains carrying these soldiers, each 54 carriages long, crossed a single bridge over the River Rhine in the first two weeks of August. The French war plan included 7000 trains taking their armies to the frontier with Germany.

ARMÉE DE TERRE ET ARMÉE DE

ORDRE DE MOBILISATION GÉNÉR

Par décret du Président de la République, la mobilisation des armées de terre et ordonnée, ainsi que la réquisition des animaux, voitures et harnais nécessaires au c de ces armées.

Le premier jour de la mobilisation est le _____

Tout Français soumis aux obligations militaires doit, sous peine d'être puni avec rigueur des lois, obéir aux prescriptions du FASCICULE DE MOBILISATION (pages placées dans son livret).

Sont visés par le présent ordre TOUS LES HOMMES non présents sous les Drap appartenant :

1° à l'ARMÉE DE TERRE y compris les TROUPES CO
SERVICES AUXILIAIRES;

2° à l'ARMÉE DE MER y
de la MARINE.

▲ *With no radio or television, posters announcing mobilisation of French forces appeared in towns and villages across the country.*

▲ *The early days of the war were a race to transport troops to the frontline before the other side could attack.*

WW1 FACTS

PALS BATTALIONS

Kitchener's new army included pals battalions. These were units filled with men from the same town or region who would serve together in the war. The first pals battalions were raised in Liverpool and many others followed, including a battalion of footballers in London.

▶ *Soldiers were recruited to Kitchener's New Army using posters like this, but they would need months of training before these volunteers were ready for battle.*

IS YOUR HOME HERE? DEFEND IT!

In contrast to the giant armies of conscripts elsewhere in Europe, Britain had a small, highly trained army. In total the army had just fewer than 250,000 regular troops but many of them were stationed across the British Empire from India to Africa. The British Expeditionary Force that was sent to fight in France and Belgium included less than 150,000 men. Lord Kitchener set about recruiting a New Army made up of volunteers. By the end of the year, more than a million men had volunteered.

"On 5 August 1914, I reported to my regimental depot... What a meeting of old friends! All were eager to take part in the great scrap that every pre-war soldier had expected."

Private R G Hill, British Army Reservist.

BATTLE OF THE FRONTIERS

The generals who plotted the vast battle plans of 1914 all expected a short war, and they all expected to be on the winning side. Germany had planned to encircle the French army and defeat them within six weeks.

Austria-Hungary was confident it could overrun little Serbia. Russia planned to invade eastern Germany and the French armies would capture the provinces that Germany had taken from them in 1871. These plans all had one thing in common: they all failed.

▲ *In the early days of the war, German cycle companies could move more quickly than troops on foot, and needed less food and other support than cavalry.*

The Belgian army was no match for more than a million German troops and the capital Brussels was soon captured. As Germany's forces pushed on towards the French border, they met determined resistance, including from the British Expeditionary Force at the Battle of Mons in France. Meanwhile, the poorly equipped French infantry, wearing brightly coloured uniforms not suited to modern warfare, was forced back from Alsace and suffered 300,000 casualties in a few weeks.

The German armies had been delayed in Belgium but they pushed on towards Paris. They were finally halted by French forces in a desperate fight at the River Marne in early September. The German forces retreated to defensive positions along high ground. The war entered a new phase.

▲ Thousands of Belgian refugees poured into France and Britain. They told terrible stories of German attacks on civilians.

▲ General Joseph Joffre was commander in chief of French forces in 1914. He planned the disastrous French offensive at the start of the war but his counter-attack at the Battle of the Marne ended German hopes of a quick victory.

WWI FACTS

WAR CRIMES

British newspapers included sensational accounts of crimes committed by German soldiers against enemy troops and civilians in Belgium. Whether they were true or not, the British government could use the stories to convince British people and other countries that Britain and her allies had right on their side. They set up an investigation into the claims and its report in 1915 repeated horrific stories of crimes against Belgian women and children, often with very little evidence.

◄ German troops march into Brussels on 22 August 1914.

DIGGING IN

The Germans were the first army to work out that the trench was a good defence against the explosive shells and machine guns of World War I but the Allies, including Britain and France, were not far behind.

Each time one army tried to attack around the edge of a line of trenches, the defenders would dig a new trench. Eventually the trenches stretched 475 miles from the borders of Switzerland to the North Sea. Despite heroic efforts on both sides they hardly moved for more than three years.

First Battle of Ypres

The British position at Ypres in Belgium jutted out into the German lines and was the scene of brutal battles for much of the war. The First Battle of Ypres began in October as the experienced British soldiers were heavily outnumbered by newly arrived German recruits.

▲ *Shovels and entrenching tools were essential equipment for those fighting on the Western Front.*

▼ *Indian soldiers, such as this cavalry division, played a vital role as part of the small British army in 1914 and 1915.*

The British were supported by Indian soldiers, unused to the rain and cold of Belgium in November. More than half of the original British Expeditionary Force had been killed or wounded by the end of this battle.

Ypres was the last major offensive of the fast-moving Battle of the Frontiers before the lines of trenches were fixed across France and Belgium. By the end of 1914, the hopes that the war would be short and glorious had disappeared completely. More than 300,000 French soldiers had been killed and German forces had suffered 241,000 deaths on the Western Front.

▲ Soldiers were issued with Christmas cards to send home. The card gave few clues about what life was like in the trenches.

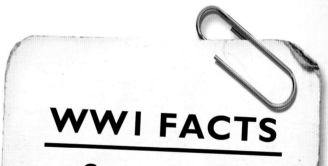

▲ Every available soldier was needed to stop the larger German forces breaking through at Ypres in November 1914.

WWI FACTS

CHRISTMAS TRUCE

On Christmas Day 1914, an unofficial truce was called. British and German soldiers emerged from their trenches to shake hands and even play football together in no man's land, the area between the two opposing trenches. One British soldier wrote in a letter:

"Just you think that whilst you were eating your turkey I was out talking with the very men I was trying to kill a few hours earlier."

TRENCH WARFARE

Trenches soon developed beyond simple ditches. The Western Front was zigzagged by complex warrens of trenches. Dugout shelters deep underground protected troops from artillery blasts.

The trenches could be defended with barbed wire and machine guns. The biggest danger was the risk that the enemy could reach the end of a trench and fire along it, although this was almost impossible with the continuous line of trenches stretching miles along the Western Front.

▲ *Trenches had to be constantly alert for attack by raiding parties armed with grenades.*

On the offensive

All armies had gone into the war believing that fast-moving cavalry would be a key attacking weapon. But horses were no match for machine guns and quick-firing artillery. The new motor vehicles were not strong or powerful enough to use in battle. New technology made a difference later in the war but until then, the only way to attack was with infantry advancing into the enemy guns. In these massed attacks, the attackers usually lost a third more men than the defenders. If they were successful they might move their frontline forward by a few hundred metres, with horrendous loss of life.

▲ *Advancing soldiers always suffered more casualties than defenders as they found what little shelter they could in no man's land.*

▶ *Millions of exploding shells and other weapons created a terrifying landscape of mud and shattered trees on the Western Front.*

▶ *Poison gas was first used by the German army on the Western Front in April 1915. Later, both sides used this terrible weapon. Gas masks were needed to protect troops from the deadly effects of gas.*

WWI FACTS

TRENCH SYSTEMS

Trench systems were very complex with frontline trenches supported by lines of reserve trenches. If a trench was overrun, the enemy would fall back to their next line of defence. Aircraft were used to take aerial photos of enemy trenches. These photos show a trench system before and after bombardment.

Before

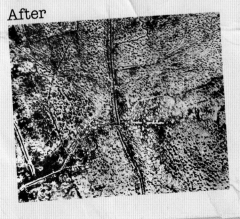

After

TRENCH LIFE

The trenches of the two sides on the Western Front were hundreds of metres apart in some places, but elsewhere there could be just a few metres of mud and barbed wire between them.

Life in the trenches for millions of men was divided between bursts of intense activity and mortal danger during attacks, with longer periods when the men tried to defeat the cold and the boredom of trench life. Trench life could go on for months without major attacks but defenders were always on their guard. Troops usually spent a few days at a time in the frontline, known as 'fire trench' where they had to be constantly alert, followed by a few days in reserve or away from the trenches. Major attacks often happened at dawn but at night there was the constant danger of raiding parties. Night-time was also when trenches were repaired and patrols sent out into no man's land.

▲ Officers could be sure that the pre-printed messages on these official postcards would stop troops from revealing military plans or secrets.

Trench conditions

Trenches were infested with rats, which thrived in the mud and slime where there was always plenty of food, including unburied dead bodies. Lice infested the clothes and hair of almost everyone. Standing in water for days on end led to illnesses such as trench foot. Whatever the horrors of trench life, the greatest danger always came when troops went 'over the top', leaving the trench to face the enemy's guns and shells head on.

▲ This postcard was sent by Private H. Giles. The photo on the front shows living conditions at the Front but behind the trenches.

▲ Troops always had to keep their equipment and helmets on in case of attack.

▲ This is a modern reconstruction of a trench. The boards on the sides stopped trench walls from collapsing.

▲ As the war dragged on, living quarters near the frontline became more permanent.

POST CARD BRITISH MADE

Correspondence

Address

Chum 17/5/15.

Dear Mr J.

Just a line to let you know that I'm still alive & am moving to King's Lynn on Wednesday next. Will write you later. How do you like photo. Best regards to the Office staff. From, H. Giles.

Mr G. Jones,
Audit Office,
G.W.R.
Paddington,
W.

▲ Canned 'bully beef' was a part of every British soldier's diet. Later in the war, rations were cut as the enemy blockade of shipping led to shortages.

BEYOND THE WESTERN FRONT

While Britain and France were mainly focused on the trench warfare of the Western Front, Germany and Austria-Hungary had to face the threat of Russia in the east. Although trench warfare eventually took over the Eastern Front, the huge distances armies had to cover in the east meant that the frontline moved many times.

▲ *German soldiers march through a Polish town that has been destroyed by retreating Russian forces.*

The Russian army started their campaign by launching a ferocious attack on eastern Germany. The poorly equipped and disorganized Russians failed to build on their success and were defeated at the Battle of Tannenberg at the end of August. By the end of 1914 the Russians had fallen back into Poland.

Freezing winter temperatures did not prevent both sides from trying to gain the upper hand in the early months of 1915. Russia had most success against the weaker Austrian army, but German reinforcements helped to drive the Russians out of Poland by the end of 1915.

The Italian front

Austria-Hungary had another problem in May 1915 when Italy joined the war against the Central Powers, as Germany and her allies were called. Italian troops attacked Austria's southern borders across the most difficult terrain of the whole war, through the icy passes of the high Alps Mountains. This new frontline used up valuable men and equipment.

▲ *Briton Flora Sandes was one of the few women to fight in the war when she became a captain in the Serbian army.*

WWI FACTS

SERBIAN RESISTANCE

Austria-Hungary had expected an easy victory over Serbia in 1914. But Serbia's soldiers were tough and experienced after engaging in war with Turkey a few years earlier. Austria's forces were repelled twice before Germany and new ally Bulgaria invaded in October 1915, forcing Serbia's force to retreat across icy mountains to safety.

Russia captured 120,000 Austro-Hungarian prisoners when the fortress of Przsemyl fell in March 1915. British observer Captain Neilson gave a damning report on the Austrian army and officers:

"I have seen [Austrian officers] sitting all day long in cafés, sleek, well fed, and complacent, while their men wander along the street, half starved and ragged, begging bread from passing Russians, who with their invariable kindness of heart always give."

▼ *Most of the Italian army came from the lowland areas of the country. They were not well suited to the challenges of fighting in the mountains.*

GALLIPOLI

As neither side could break the deadlock on the Western Front, Allied commanders looked for other ways to attack the Central Powers. The Turkish Ottoman Empire had joined Germany and Austria-Hungary in October 1914 and looked like a soft target for attack.

Landing troops from the sea was very risky but many powerful voices, including the minister for the Royal Navy Winston Churchill, argued that the plan might just work.

On 25 April 1915, several weeks after an unsuccessful naval attack, troops from France and the British Empire, including thousands from Australia and New Zealand, landed at two points on the Gallipoli peninsula. The troops found themselves fighting for their lives on heavily defended beaches and could make little progress. After months of bloody combat, most Allied troops were evacuated at the end of 1915.

Allies together

The fighting at Gallipoli cost more than 100,000 lives including 66,000 Turkish defenders, 28,000 British, 10,000 French and 10,000 soldiers from Australia and New Zealand (called the ANZACs). This is just one example of the massive contribution that soldiers from the British Empire made to the Allied war effort. British Empire forces also included 1.5 million Indians, who played a vital part in the war in the Middle East.

The disaster of Gallipoli convinced the Allied generals even more that their efforts should be concentrated on the Western Front, although a base set up at Salonika in Greece would help to open another front later in the war.

"On the first day, we were just mixed up and running around like a lot of rabbits. – nobody could see who was who or what was what. And it was [when we were evacuated from the line] for the first time we realized what the taking of Anzac Ridge had cost, because hardly any of our mates were left."

Australian Private Frank Brent describes the confusion of the landing at Gallipoli in April.

This extract from a report was written by Sir Ian Hamilton, Allied commander at Gallipoli. It gives his first impressions of how the campaign was going. Things were not going to plan.

"Gallipoli looks a much tougher nut to crack than it did over the map in my office."

Hamilton's planning and leadership was criticized in the official report into Gallipoli.

◀ Soldiers of the Lancashire Fusiliers prepare to land on the heavily defended beaches of Gallipoli.

▲ The fierce defence of Gallipoli by Turkish forces forced the Allies to change their plans.

THE WIDER WORLD

From the start, the war's reach extended far beyond the borders of Europe to the empires of the warring nations. The soldiers of this war included two million Africans, fighting in or supporting the armies of Britain, France and Germany as they battled over their African colonies.

When the Ottoman Empire joined the fight, the deserts of the Middle East became an important battleground.

Africa

Almost all of the continent of Africa had been divided up between European powers in the decades before 1914. Britain asked its own colonies and the dominion of South Africa to seize German possessions. Some, such as Togoland, fell quickly but German East Africa actually resisted longer than Germany itself.

▲ *Those armies in the Middle East had to deal with scorching desert heat as well as defeating the enemy.*

The Middle East

The war in Mesopotamia, which is now called Iraq, lasted from October 1914 to the end of the war. At first British and Indian forces made good progress in the difficult desert terrain. However, Turkish forces fought back and thousands of Allied soldiers died in the 147-day siege of Kut al-Amara, or became prisoners when they finally surrendered.

▲ *T. E. Lawrence chose Arab dress as he used the Arabs' wish for independence from the Ottoman Empire to help the Allied war effort.*

British forces also fought the Turks in Sinai and Palestine. Their main aim was to protect the Suez Canal, through which ships brought troops and supplies from India and Australia. British generals also decided to push on for victory in Palestine. General Sir Edmund Allenby led a successful campaign in 1917 and 1918 supported by an Arab revolt inspired by British officer T. E. Lawrence, known as Lawrence of Arabia.

Many Africans were forced by their leaders to join the war. They knew very little about why they were fighting. An African recruit remembers how he ended up as a carrier for British forces:

"We came back one night from our yam farm. The chief called us and handed us over to a government messenger. I didn't know where we were going, but the chief and the messenger said that the white man had sent for us and we must go."

▲ Egypt was a vital base for Allied troops because of the importance of the Suez Canal.

THE BATTLES OF 1916

On the Western Front, generals looked for new ways to break the deadlock. To make a decisive break in the trenches, they needed vast numbers of men and munitions.

▲ The land around Verdun was so devastated by months of fighting that many towns and villages were never rebuilt.

The British army needed time for hundreds of thousands of recruits to be trained and for industry to produce the guns and explosives the Allies needed. There were attempts to break through in 1915 but it was 1916 when two colossal battles pushed both sides close to exhaustion.

WWI FACTS

WAR HORSES

Horses pulled the heavy artillery guns across ground that had been churned up and blasted by shells. Thousands of horses lost their lives in the battles of Verdun and the Somme.

Verdun

On 21 February 1916, Germany launched an offensive on French forces around the fortresses of Verdun. Germany knew that France would give anything, including heavy losses, to protect this key stronghold. In a horrific battle that lasted until December, Germany and France suffered more than 700,000 casualties between them as a whole area was pulverized by artillery. The landscape was changed forever as forests and villages were wiped from the map by millions of shells.

▶ This painting captures the bleak mud of the Somme battlefield after months of fighting back and forth across the same few kilometres of ground.

WAR DIARY
or
INTELLIGENCE SUMMARY
(Erase heading not required.)

ding War Diaries and Intelligence
re contained in F. S. Regs, Part II.
f Manual respectively. Title Pages
ared in manuscript.

Remarks and
references to
Appendices

Summary of Events and Information

Date	Hour		
ly 4th.	A.M. 7'37	Adjutant,14th Brigade R.H.A. reports that guns have been ordered to barrage a line 300 yards North of a line running E and W through most Northern house in BAZENTIN LE PETIT.	
	7'55	O.P. D/14 reports Infantry massing behind HIGH WOOD.	
	11'45	Brigadier General Seely called at Brigade H.Q. states "Canadian Cavalry Brigade behind POMMIERS REDOUBT and one troop South of MAMETZ WOOD. At 10'45 a.m. 1 Regiment (7th D.G.) Secunderabad Cavalry Brigade was seen by General Seely South of MAMETZ WOOD.	
	P.M. 12'5	22nd Infantry Brigade report a large number of enemy advancing from HIGH WOOD.	
	12'10	Enemy attacking CEMETERY and WINDMILL. Divisional Artillery shooting at them with observed fire	
	12'55	Lieut Morshead, Brigade Signal Officer, returns from BAZENTIN LE GRAND and brought back sketches from 8th Devon Regt and 2nd Border Regt.	
	3.	Our infantry seen on WINDMILL HILL Ridge. Situation appreciated that 2 battalions 22nd Infantry Brigade were carrying out an attack towards HIGH WOOD.	
	3'45	"T" Battery reports message intercepted "Enemy advancing from HIGH WOOD".	
	5.	Lieut LAWLEY, 20th M.G.Coy reports the situation.	
	6'20	Major DOBSON, 95th Field Coy,R.E. reports the original Brigade objective strongly consolidated at the strong points detailed in orders.	
	6'25	Situation reported to 7th Division.	
	6'45	2nd Gordon Highlanders reported by 22nd Infantry Brigade to be holding 200 yards N.of BAZENTIN LE PETIT VILLAGE,and in BAZENTIN LE PETIT WOOD.	

◀ *War diaries told the official story of the war. This diary dates from 14 July 1916, two weeks after the start of the Battle of the Somme. It talks about attacks and other incidents but does not include personal details of those who fought in the war.*

The Somme

French and British forces had been planning a major offensive around the Somme valley for many months. Britain's volunteer army were now battle ready and the British government had also introduced conscription to force men to join the army. With these troops and more than three million shells ready for use, they hoped to overwhelm the German defenders. When the attack was launched on 1 July 1916, it would also help to distract the enemy from the bloody struggle at Verdun.

After the catastrophic losses of the first day, the two sides traded blows and casualties for five months until the battle was finally called off on 19 November. There were around 600,000 casualties on each side in the battle. These included more than 400,000 British casualties, many of whom had been part of the pals battalions who had volunteered in the early months of the war. This terrible slaughter had enabled the Allies to move forward 12 kilometres at the furthest point. There was no decisive breakthrough.

TREATING THE WOUNDED

Before 1914, most deaths in wartime were caused by disease rather than enemy weapons. That changed in World War I as high explosives and machine guns could inflict terrible injuries. Medical knowledge was still basic by modern standards.

Medical services were overwhelmed by the numbers and severity of injuries during the war. Apart from the effects of blasts and bullets, one of the major risks was that wounds could become infected. Antibiotics to prevent infection had not yet been discovered. Casualties were treated in the frontline before being transferred to field hospitals away from the trenches. Seriously injured soldiers would then be transferred to hospitals nearer home.

Shell shock

The horrors of the Western Front led to terrible mental injuries as well as physical ones. Shell shock was the name given to mental illness and breakdowns caused by the strain of warfare. The British army dealt with around 80,000 cases of shell shock, but ordinary soldiers were often forced to return to the frontline. More than 300 British soldiers were court martialled and executed for refusing to fight, many were suffering from shell shock.

Plastic surgery

Many soldiers suffered terrible facial injuries during the war. Dr Harold Gillies led a medical team who developed new medical techniques called plastic surgery to reconstruct disfigured faces.

▲ A hospital train evacuates seriously injured soldiers to hospitals in their home country.

◀ Horse-drawn
ambulances were still
common in World
War I.

◀ Horse-drawn
ambulances were still
common in World
War I.

PROCEEDINGS OF A MEDICAL BOARD

Army Form A. 45.

CONFIDENTIAL.

Assembled at. *Exchange Hotel Liverpool* on *July 20th 1917*

By order of *G.O.C. of Western Comd.*

For the purpose of examining and reporting upon the present state of health of

(Rank and Name) *2nd Lt Siegfried Sassoon* (Corps)

Age *30* Service *2 yrs* Disability *Mental Break Down*

Date of commencement of leave granted for present disability

Date on which placed on half-pay for present disability

The Board having assembled pursuant to order, and having read the instructions on the back of the form, proceed to examine the above-named officer and find that

*his mental condition is abnormal. his
conversation is disconnected and somewhat
irrational. his manner nervous and
excitable. In addition to this his family history
is neuropathic: He is suffering from a
nervous breakdown and we do not
consider him responsible for his actions
this officer may be examined by any
Board*

The opinion of the Board upon the questions herein is as follows:—

(1.) a. Is the officer fit for "General Service"?
    b. If not so fit, how long is he likely to be unfit?
(2.) a. If unfit for General Service, is he fit for service at home?
    b. If not so fit, how long is he likely to be unfit for service at home?
    c. If unfit for General Service at home, is he fit for light duty at home?
    d. If not so fit, how long is he likely to be unfit for light duty at home?
(3.) Was the disability contracted in the service? *Yes*
(4.) Was it contracted under circumstances over which he had } *Yes*
    no control?
(5.) Was it caused by military service? *Yes*
(6.) If caused by military service, } *Strain of active service. being*
    to what specific conditions } *of a nervous temperament*
    is it attributed?
(7.) If the disability was not caused by military } *No*
    service, was it aggravated by it?

W Alexander Lt.Col. RamC.T. President.

Signatures { *Cui si Dow an Calfraini* } Members.

[P.T.O.

Form...

◀ Poet Siegfried
Sassoon volunteered
shortly after the
outbreak of war.
He received the
British Military
Cross medal for
his bravery on the
Western Front. In
July 1917 he failed
to report for duty
after being on sick
leave because of
a shoulder injury.
This is the report
of the medical
board, which
concluded that
he was suffering
from shell shock
and was not
responsible for
his actions.

HOME FRONTS

World War I was a 'total war'. Success did not just depend on the strength of the armies but also on the factories that supplied the shells, uniforms, boots and all the other things needed by millions of soldiers.

▲ *These stamps were used by Germans to claim their small ration of bread.*

During the war, British forces on the Western Front were supplied with more than five million tonnes of munitions and three million tonnes of food. The whole population of the warring nations had a role to play in the war effort.

Early in the war, governments started to take control of important industries such as the railways or factories that could be used to make war equipment. At that time, people expected a short war but as the conflict wore on, governments took more and more control.

WWI FACTS

WAR BREAD

Germans added other ingredients to make their food go further. 'War bread' included potatoes and sometimes even straw.

RATIONAL SERVICE

JOHN BULL. "SACRIFICE INDEED! WHY, I'M FEELING FITTER EVERY MINUTE, AND I'VE STILL PLENTY OF WEIGHT TO SPARE."

Reproduced by the special permission of the Proprietors of "Punch,"

And published by the Ministry of Food.

ADOPT VOLUNTARY RATIONS.

Shortages and starvation

Both sides tried to stop supplies reaching the enemy with naval blockades and attacks on merchant shipping. In Britain this led to rationing and queues for some essential foods and coal later in the war. In Germany and Austria-Hungary the situation became very serious as civilians had to make do with terrible rations because the Allies prevented food reaching them. More than 700,000 people in Central Europe died from starvation by the end of the war.

◀ *This poster from Britain's Ministry of Food encouraged people to voluntarily change their diet so there would be more food to go round.*

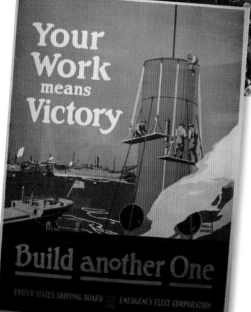

◀ Stories about spying and atrocities in Belgium led to many attacks on supposed Germans in London and elsewhere. Many families and businesses with German names had been in Britain for generations.

◀ All warring nations, including the United States, used posters and advertising to persuade people to work harder for the war effort.

WWI FACTS

THE DEFENCE OF THE REALM ACT

The Defence of the Realm Act gave the British government special powers during the war, including the right to court martial anyone passing information to the enemy or spreading "false reports or reports likely to cause disaffection to His Majesty or to interfere with the success of His Majesty's force's by land or sea."

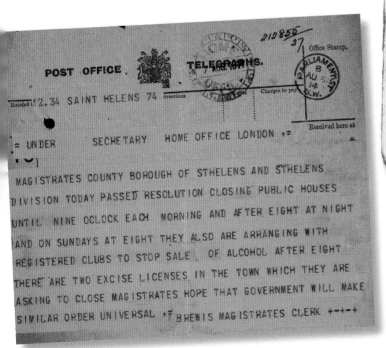

POST OFFICE TELEGRAPHS.

Handed 12.34 SAINT HELENS 74

UNDER SECRETARY HOME OFFICE LONDON

MAGISTRATES COUNTY BOROUGH OF STHELENS AND STHELENS
DIVISION TODAY PASSED RESOLUTION CLOSING PUBLIC HOUSES
UNTIL NINE OCLOCK EACH MORNING AND AFTER EIGHT AT NIGHT
AND ON SUNDAYS AT EIGHT THEY ALSO ARE ARRANGING WITH
REGISTERED CLUBS TO STOP SALE OF ALCOHOL AFTER EIGHT
THERE ARE TWO EXCISE LICENSES IN THE TOWN WHICH THEY ARE
ASKING TO CLOSE MAGISTRATES HOPE THAT GOVERNMENT WILL MAKE
SIMILAR ORDER UNIVERSAL BREWIS MAGISTRATES CLERK

◀ New rules restricted daily life. The government followed St Helen's magistrates in limiting the sale of alcohol to make sure people were ready for work in the morning.

UNDER ATTACK

On 19 January 1915, Great Yarmouth was the first British town to experience a new menace – the Zeppelin. These airships had already dropped bombs on Paris and other French towns.

These huge but almost silent balloons often attacked on clear, dark nights. It was Britain's first experience of being attacked from the air. Before the first Zeppelin attack, German warships had already bombarded ports on the east coast of Britain. In 1917, slow-moving Zeppelins were replaced by Gotha aircraft. In total, 1413 people were killed by air raids in Britain during the war.

▲ *A Zeppelin brings terror to the skies over London in 1915.*

While the death toll was tiny when compared to the losses on the frontline, attacks on civilians led to fierce hatred of the enemy. In revenge, British aircraft bombed German targets in 1918, including factories in the Ruhr and Rhineland. The German capital Berlin escaped attack as it was too distant for Allied aircraft to reach.

◄ *Posters like this were put up in public places to help people identify enemy aircraft.*

Refugees

Civilians in other countries faced greater dangers than most people in Britain. In Belgium and northern France, local residents were forced from their homes or had to live under enemy occupation. More than 250,000 Belgian refugees fled to Britain in 1914. On the Eastern Front, towns and villages were often destroyed or changed hands more than once during the war.

Governments targeted population groups who were thought to side with the enemy. In Britain, thousands of Germans and Austrians were locked up in camps during the war. Armenian people in the Ottoman Empire faced terrible revenge after Armenian nationalists sided with Russia. More than a million Armenian men, women, and children were murdered, often being marched into the desert without food and water.

▲ Many French and Belgian towns close to the frontline, such as the ancient city of Reims, were ruined by artillery fire.

▼ A crashed Gotha aircraft is displayed in a French town square.

WOMEN AT WORK

The war brought many changes to the lives of women in all warring nations. The 'total war' effort meant that industries and farms needed to keep working even though the men who had traditionally done these jobs were away at war.

Millions of women already worked in factories or as domestic servants but the outbreak of war opened up new opportunities. Women were now employed in a range of new jobs from office workers to bus drivers.

Many young women also trained as nurses. The numbers of wounded soldiers meant that buildings such as large country houses were converted into hospitals. British Voluntary Aid Detachments (VADs) and First Aid Nursing Yeomanry (FANYs) served as nurses and ambulance drivers close to the frontline. Driving an ambulance could be a very dangerous job as casualties had to be transported under fire.

▲ *Bricklaying was just one of the jobs that women workers took on during wartime.*

Women on the frontline

There was more opposition to women serving in other roles at the frontline. By 1917, the armies needed all available men to fight. The British army formed the Women's Army Auxiliary Corps to support troops at the front doing jobs such as cooking. By 1918, 40,000 women had joined the WAAC, which changed its name to the Queen Mary's Army Auxiliary Corps, and 7000 had faced the dangers of life on the Western Front.

WWI FACTS

ANGELS UNDER FIRE

Elsie Knocker and Mairi Chisholm were known as the 'Angels of Pervyse'. They saved the lives of countless soldiers from their first-aid post close to the frontline in Belgium, while surviving artillery shells and sniper fire.

▶ This picture shows the arm badge that WLA volunteers wore.

NATIONAL SERVICE

"GERMANY" MEANS TO STARVE US OUT THERE IS ONLY ONE ANSWER A BLOW STRAIGHT BETWEEN THE EYES NATIONAL SERVICE CAN DEAL THAT BLOW"
Mr NEVILLE CHAMBERLAIN, Director-General.

ENROL TO-DAY AND RELEASE A FIT MAN FOR THE FRONT

FORMS FOR OFFER OF SERVICES MAY BE HAD AT ALL POST OFFICES NATIONAL SERVICE OFFICES AND EMPLOYMENT EXCHANGES

▲ In 1915, there were fewer women working on farms than there had been before the war, mainly because of new job opportunities elsewhere. In Britain, the Women's Land Army was started in February 1917 to provide workers for agriculture, which were essential for food production.

▶ As more men were killed and wounded, pressure rose on women to replace men on the home front.

NATIONAL SERVICE.

"One clear Call for me."

EVERY GIRL WHO ENLISTS IN THE W.A.A.C. Releases a Man for the **B.E.F.** (British Expeditionary Forces).

Women and girls who have reached the age of 20 are required at once to do **general clerical work** at the bases in France. Shorthand and Typewriting not essential. **Cooks, Waitresses, Housemaids**, Strong Women for **Bakehouse, Scrubbers** and **Laundresses**, are also needed for service in France. Successful candidates will wear khaki uniform, live in hostels under comfortable conditions, and receive payment at fixed rates. Also **1,000 Domestic Workers**, all classes, are wanted for immediate service in Military Camps at **Home**.

HELP the MEN to FIGHT!

Application Forms and Conditions of Service can be obtained from

Miss WOODGATE, National Service Commissioner, 21, Bond Street, LEEDS.

Women engaged in Government Departments or controlled firms should only apply with the written consent of their employers.

▲ This advert for the WAAC lists a range of jobs for women in France, from general office work to "scrubbers and laundresses".

▶ Members of the Women's Army Auxiliary Corps prepare a meal for troops in France.

MUNITIONS FACTORIES

By spring 1915, there was a 'shell crisis' on the Western Front. Britain and France were not producing enough artillery shells to feed the thousands of guns that bombarded enemy trenches.

At one point in 1915, British guns were restricted to firing four shells per day. Something had to be done or the war would be lost. A new Ministry of Munitions started building vast factories to supply the shells and bullets their armies needed. By 1917, Britain could produce 50 million shells per year, compared to just 500,000 in 1914. France's munitions industry could produce even more. The Central Powers could not keep up with this speed of production.

Dangerous work

The workers in these munitions factories were often women. Pay was good compared to many other jobs, but the hours were long and the work was very dangerous. In 1917, an explosion at the Silvertown munitions factory in London killed 69 people, and damaged more than 70,000 houses in the surrounding area.

▲ *Recruiting posters like this one encouraged workers to believe that they were doing their bit for the country's war effort. They did not show the health problems that affected many munitions workers.*

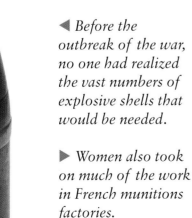

◄ *Before the outbreak of the war, no one had realized the vast numbers of explosive shells that would be needed.*

► *Women also took on much of the work in French munitions factories.*

▲ *Strict regulations were needed to protect munitions workers who were surrounded by high explosives.*

Danger! High explosive

Trinitrotoluene, or TNT, was the explosive material used in shells. This document includes detailed rules for those working with TNT. The length of the document alone shows just how dangerous TNT was. It was particularly important to stay clean and wear a uniform in the factory so this lethal explosive could not be carried on their clothes. As well as the danger from explosions, long exposure to TNT caused workers' skin and hair to turn yellow. In extreme cases it caused death and more than 100 women died from TNT poisoning.

G. R.

RULES FOR THE USE OF TRINITROTOLUENE.

Issued by THE MINISTRY OF MUNITIONS.

PROPAGANDA

In spite of the terrible losses and hardships of the war, only a small number of people openly called for an end to the conflict. People of all the warring nations were constantly fed government propaganda, which encouraged them to support the war.

▲ *Rudyard Kipling composed patriotic poems and stories about the war, although he lost his son John at the Battle of Loos in 1915.*

Propaganda is information that is designed to support a particular view. All governments tried to convince ordinary civilians and soldiers that they were fighting a just war. British and French newspapers printed lurid stories of German crimes in Belgium. In turn, Germany accused the Allies of mistreating prisoners. These stories presented the war as a battle between good and evil, and were designed to help justify the deaths of hundreds of thousands of young men in battle. Reports from the frontline were censored to show the best possible side of events. It was important not to give information to the enemy but also to hide the horrors of the war from civilians.

▲ *Newspaper editors were an important part of official propaganda. Most reports from the frontline were approved by the government.*

War Propaganda Bureau

The official view of the war entered many areas of life beyond the newspapers. The British War Propaganda Bureau produced books, films and other materials about the war.

▶ *In a time before radio or television broadcasting, people relied on newspapers for the latest news about the war.*

The **CLEANEST** fighter in the World—the British Tommy

The clean, chivalrous fighting instincts of our gallant soldiers reflect the ideals of our business life. The same characteristics which stamp the British Tommy as the *CLEANEST FIGHTER IN THE WORLD* have won equal repute for British Goods.

SUNLIGHT SOAP is typically British. It is acknowledged by experts to represent the highest standard of Soap Quality and Efficiency. Tommy welcomes it in the trenches just as you welcome it at home.

£1,000 GUARANTEE OF PURITY ON EVERY BAR.

The name Lever on Soap is a Guarantee of Purity and Excellence.

LEVER BROTHERS LIMITED, PORT SUNLIGHT.

▲ *Adverts, like this one for Sunlight Soap, were desperate to link their product with heroic soldiers at the Front.*

Musicians and writers spread the patriotic spirit and there were all kinds of products such as china figures of Lord Kitchener. One youngster wrote to her father at the front to tell him about the trench scene that was part of a Liverpool Christmas grotto.

Posters and pamphlets urged people to put all their effort into winning the war, whether by working harder than the enemy or buying war bonds to help pay for the conflict. By the end of the war, a new Ministry of Information was created to control all these propaganda efforts.

WWI FACTS

FILM PROPAGANDA

Cinema was the newest media channel and the authorities did not ignore its power. Propaganda films such as *The Battle of the Somme* were watched by millions of people.

NO HOLIDAYS

"Fritz! Fritz! are those British munition workers never going to take a holiday!"

▲ *This poster convinced munitions workers that by taking no holidays they were helping the war effort.*

OPPOSING THE WAR

Propaganda could not convince everyone to support the war. In 1914, opponents were drowned out by the popular support for war but this gradually changed, particularly after the British government introduced conscription, forcing all men aged between 18 and 41 to join the armed forces from May 1916.

Socialists and many of those campaigning for women's rights believed strongly in international solidarity rather than fighting against other nations.

▲ Before conscription, propaganda targeted those men who had not yet joined the armed forces.

Conscientious objectors

In other countries, conscription had been in place before the war but Britain had maintained an army of professional soldiers and volunteers. After 1914, young men who did not volunteer or were not wearing military uniform often faced insults and scorn in public but they did not legally have to fight. When conscription was introduced, most of the thousands of conscientious objectors accepted other war work but 843 were given prison sentences for refusing to serve at all. Ten of these conscientious objectors died in prison.

▶ Men who had not volunteered to fight, or were not wearing uniform, risked being handed a white feather by a woman as a sign of cowardice.

◀ Conscientious objectors stage a peace demonstration in 1917.

▶ This letter was sent by the father of conscientious objector James Scott Duckers after the end of the war, begging for his son's release from prison. Mr Duckers' daughter had been killed while serving as a nurse in the war.

Easter Rising

Some groups had their own reasons for opposing the war. In April 1916 a small group of rebels staged a revolt in Dublin to gain Irish independence from Britain. They had been promised German support but the Easter Rising was quickly and ruthlessly ended by British troops. The brutal actions of the battle-hardened British soldiers helped to strengthen Irish resistance to British rule and led to an independent Irish state just five years later.

▼ Dublin's General Post Office building was the scene of fierce clashes during the Easter Rising.

WWI FACTS

MUTINY IN FRANCE

In spring 1917, French soldiers were driven into opposition to the war by a disastrous offensive on the Chemin des Dames. Around 40,000 soldiers in 68 divisions of the French army refused to mount any more attacks. Elsewhere in France, workers went on strike to protest against the war and high food prices. French generals made concessions to calm the mutinies but it was clear that, in France, there was little appetite for war after years of bloodshed.

THE WAR AT SEA

The biggest battles of World War I were fought on the Western and Eastern Fronts, but control of the oceans was a matter of life and death for both sides. The British Royal Navy blockaded Germany to prevent food and supplies reaching the Central Powers. Germany also had a secret weapon of her own: the U-boat.

▲ *This postage stamp was printed to remember the sinking of the Lusitania.*

The British Royal Navy was the most powerful force on the oceans. The German fleet was smaller and its best chances lay in luring small groups of British ships into battle. However, at the end of May 1916, the German High Seas Fleet eventually left port. The British were ready. The two fleets met at the Battle of Jutland. The Germans sunk more British ships and claimed victory, but Britain still had a much bigger fleet. The German fleet never challenged their enemy again.

▼ *The Battle of Jutland was the largest battle of surface ships in history, with just under 100 German ships facing more than 150 British ships.*

WWI FACTS

RMS LUSITANIA

The sinking of the passenger ship Lusitania off the coast of Ireland in 1915 was one of the biggest scandals of the war. 1201 passengers and crew died including many Americans. Germany claimed that the ship was carrying munitions, making it a target for attack. In 2008, a remote-controlled submarine vehicle discovered a large cargo of bullets inside the ship's wreck.

▲ *Captain Schwieger, the commander of the U-boat that torpedoed the Lusitania.*

Submarine warfare

Germany had more success with its submarine, or U-boat, fleet. Britain and France also had submarines but German U-boats were most effective during the war, attacking warships and merchant ships to prevent troops and supplies reaching the Allies from overseas. Germany had no more than 140 U-boats in service at any time, but in 1917 they sank 2439 Allied and neutral ships.

On 1 February 1917, Germany declared unrestricted submarine warfare on Allied and neutral ships, meaning that ships would be sunk without warning. Attacks on their ships pushed the USA to declare war, joining the Allied side in April 1917.

▲ *Life at sea was much more dangerous than suggested by the blue skies of this recruiting poster.*

THE WESTERN FRONT IN 1917

By 1917, all countries were showing signs of exhaustion from the war. France was still reeling from the carnage of Verdun and the Somme when General Nivelle launched his disastrous attack on the Chemin des Dames in April 1917.

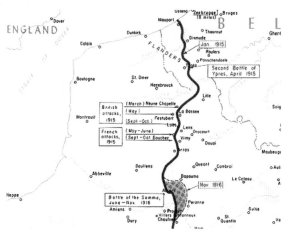

▲ *This map shows the northern section of the Western Front that moved little between late 1914 and the start of 1918.*

If that was not bad enough, after a successful offensive by General Brusilov against Austria-Hungary in 1916, Russia's tsar, or emperor, had been deposed by revolution in March 1917. Britain would have to bear the brunt of the Allied war effort in 1917.

Passchendaele

On 31 July 1917, the British army launched the Third Battle of Ypres across the marshy land of Belgium where so much fighting had taken place. The Allies were to attack the high ground

▲ *Stretcher bearers struggle through the deep mud during the Battle of Passchendaele.*

around the village of Passchendaele. Exploding shells and heavy rain turned the terrain they had to cross into a swamp. British, Canadian and ANZAC soldiers battled through the mud and German defences for months. They eventually reached the ruined village of Passchendaele but at a huge cost with countless dead and wounded troops, including many who drowned in flooded shell craters.

WWI FACTS

MINES AT MESSINES

At dawn on 7 June 1917, a thunderous explosion on the Messines Ridge near Ypres was heard as far away as London. The blast was the detonation of mines packed into tunnels beneath the German lines. Around 10,000 German soldiers died in the blast.

▲ *The crater left by the mine explosion at Messines measured more than 100 metres across and was 45 metres deep.*

ALION OF THE ... BY COLONEL L.H.HANBURY V.D., C.M.G. COMMANDING.

No 63.   28th September 1916.

DECORATIONS.
The G.O.C.-in-C. has made the following awards:-
T/ Lieut Colonel H.T. Dobbin 8th R.War.R.
AR to the DISTINGUISHED SERVICE ORDER;
T/ Brig-General G.C. Sladen D.S.O.,M.C.
Comndg. 143rd INF.BDE.

DENTITY DISCS.
Army Routine Order No 49 dated 11th July 1916 is republished
or information:-
"It has come to notice that sufficient care is not being
ken by Officers and Men to wear their identity Discs at all times.
"All ranks are warned that it is their duty to do so on all
casions."

AVE -MEDICAL INSPECTION OF N.C.O's AND MEN PROCEEDING ON.
Before proceeding on leave all N.C.O's and men should be furn-
ed with a certificate signed by a Medical Officer stating
t they are not suffering from any infectious or contagious
ease.

AGE TO CROPS.
Care is to be taken during training to avoid damaging crops
frightening cattle especially these that are tethered.

RLY OFFICER.
2/Lieut E.B.Mitford will perform the duties of Orderly Officer
to-morrow 29/9/16.

        NOTICES.

A Boxing Competition will be held by the 1/5th Bn.Gloucester
ent, on Sunday,1st October,1916, commencing 2-30 p.m. in a
on the VACQUERIE - BERNAVILLE Road.
he following N.C.O's and Men of the 1/5th Gloucester Regt are
red to box all commers in the Division on the weights given:-
Sergt Pepperill   Heavy Weight.
Pte Jay.   Between 11st.4lbs and 10st.4lbs.
/Cpl Hobbs   -do- 11st.2lbs and 10st.2lbs.
ergt Reeves)
rivate Doyle)   -do- 10st.8lbs.and 9st.8lbs.

PRIZES.   Winner 50 francs. CONDITIONS.Six 2 Minute
          Loser 20 francs. rounds with 6oz gloves.

lications to enter this competition should be submitted
time to O.C. 1/5th Bn. Gloucestershire Regt.

                (Signed) V.C. Holland 2/Lieut&A/Adjt.
1/7th Bn. Royal Warwickshire Regiment.

Lions led by donkeys?

Historians have questioned whether commanders were too ready to risk the lives of their men in attacks like the one at Passchendaele. The soldiers have been described as "lions led by donkeys". The armies of all sides had to adapt to the weapons and tactics of modern warfare. British Field-Marshal Sir Douglas Haig, the commander who sent thousands of troops to their deaths in the Somme and Passchendaele was able to change tactics for the victorious battles of 1918.

◀ *These orders were sent out to troops in the field. Along with details of a boxing competition and warnings not to trample on crops, all men are ordered to wear identity discs at all times.*

▶ *Although French commander Joffre (second from left) was replaced after the disaster of Verdun, Douglas Haig (third from left) led British forces until the end of the war.*

NEW WEAPONS

Advances in weapons and technology played a decisive role in the war. Machine guns and powerful artillery led to the deadlock of trench warfare as they could not be overcome by massed attacks of infantry and cavalry. New weapons also played a big part in breaking the stalemate on the Western Front.

Tank triumph?

Ernest Swinton, an officer in the British Royal Engineers, had developed an idea in late 1914 for an armoured vehicle that could attack trenches. The first tanks rumbled across the Somme battlefield in late 1916. Although useless in the mud of Passchendaele, 324 British tanks were able to win territory at the Battle of Cambrai in November 1917. Maybe the new tanks, although they were slow and unreliable, could spell an end to trench warfare.

▲ *This photo from January 1916 shows one of the first tanks, called Big Willie or Mother Tank, being tested in secret.*

Air power

The Wright Brothers made their first powered flight just 11 years before the outbreak of war. Between 1914 and 1918, military aircraft changed dramatically. In 1914 aircraft could only really be used for reconnaissance of enemy positions.

Technical developments such as guns that could fire through a plane's propeller led to ace fighter pilots battling for supremacy over the Western Front. The balance of power changed

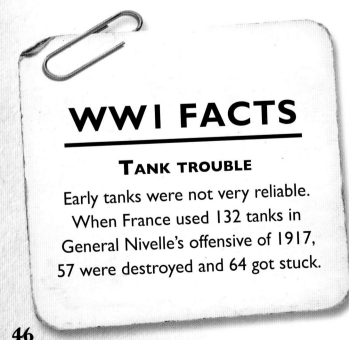

WWI FACTS

TANK TROUBLE

Early tanks were not very reliable. When France used 132 tanks in General Nivelle's offensive of 1917, 57 were destroyed and 64 got stuck.

◀ *This triplane is the same as the one flown by the brilliant 'Red Baron' Manfred von Richthofen, the most famous fighter ace of the war.*

▼ *Early in the war, aircraft were largely used for surveillance and photographing enemy trenches and troop movements.*

with each new invention. These dogfights created heroes such as Britain's Albert Ball and Germany's feared 'Red Baron' Manfred von Richthofen, but their heroics did not win or lose the war's major battles.

By 1918, air power was starting to have a big impact on the war. Large groups of aircraft could bomb enemy positions and support attacks. At this time, the Allies were able to produce more than five times as many aircraft as Germany.

▲ *Machine guns first appeared in the 1800s, but advances in technology made them much more reliable during World War I.*

WAR IN WORDS

Many of the words written about World War I were written in support of the war, either because of the writer's own beliefs or as wartime propaganda. Britain's War Propaganda Bureau used famous writers such as Arthur Conan Doyle and HG Wells to get across the patriotic view of the war.

But the voices that bring the trenches to life can be found in the verses and novels of the young writers who fought and often died in the war.

War poets

The poems of Rupert Brooke reflect the optimism of the early months of the war. Brooke died in 1915 on his way to the Dardanelles. Later in the war, and particularly after the Battle of the Somme, poets like Siegfried Sassoon, Isaac Rosenberg and Wilfred Owen wrote verse that was anti-war and tried to capture the experience of trench warfare.

The horrible reality of the trenches inspired other forms of art besides poetry. German soldier Erich Maria Remarque's *All Quiet on the Western Front* is one of the most powerful novels of the war. Artists too were sent to record the war, often for use in propaganda, although the authorities were not always happy with the images that artists created.

▲ *The boredom of trench life gave writers time to record their experiences.*

▼ *The painting* Gassed *by John Singer Sargent shows the effects of a gas attack.*

FIELD SERVICE.

F.NO.
AL14056

RT of Death of an Officer to be forwarded to the War Office with the least possible delay after receipt of notification of death on Army Form B. 213 or Army Form A. 36 or from other official documentary sources.

9/03/2218

ENT   2nd Bn MANCHESTER REGT.   Squadron, Troop, Battery or Company

T.F.

C.S.(A.L.)

2/Lt.

OWEN, W.E.S.

By whom reported   O.C. Bn.   25/11/18.

Date of Death   xxxxxxxxx   4/11/18.

Place or Hospital   France.

Cause of Death   Killed in Action.

Place of Burial   ------

whether he leaves a will or not   Not received.

All private documents and effects received from the front or hospital, should be examined, and if any will is found it should be at once forwarded to the War Office.
          Not received.

Any information received as to verbal expressions by a deceased Officer of his wishes as to the disposal of his estate should be reported to the War Office as soon as possible.
          Not received.

Signature of Officer in charge of Section Adjutant-General's Office at the Base.   L R Chapman   Capt., for
          Officer i/c Infantry Section, No. 6, G.H.Q., 3rd Echelon, B.E.F.

ion and Date 11/11/18.

4 Advanced Section, A. P. & S. S., 428, 90000, 9/17.

◄ *Wilfred Owen's only volume of poetry was published by Siegfried Sassoon in 1930. The two had met in hospital during the war. Wilfred Owen was killed in action one week before the end of the conflict. This is the official report of his death.*

▶ *Wilfred Owen*

Personal & Confidential   20th. July. 1918.

Dear Sir,

Attention has been drawn to some verses on p. 394 of your issue of the 13th. July, 1918, signed by Siegfried Sassoon. Presumably, therefore, the author is Captain S. L. Sassoon, M.C., of the 3rd. Bn. Royal Welsh Fusiliers.

This Officer in July 1917, was reported by a medical board to be suffering from a nervous breakdown and not responsible for his actions, but at the end of November, 1917, he was found to have recovered and to be fit for General Service. He is now serving in France.

Your Reviewer on p. 400 of the same issue recognises clearly what was the state of Mr. Sassoon's mind when he wrote "Counter-attack and other Poems", but if Capt. Sassoon were now writing verse such as that printed on p. 394, it would appear that his mind is still chaos, and that he is not fit to be trusted with mens' lives. I should therefore be grateful if you would let me know when you received his verses "I stood with the dead". It may be, of course, that they have been in your possession some months. The information, which is desired solely in the public interest, will of course be treated as confidential.

Yours faithfully,

A.W. Marsinel.   (Sgd) George Cox V...

◄ *This letter gives a fascinating glimpse of what the military authorities thought of some of the poetry being written in the trenches. The writer suggests that a published poem by Siegfried Sassoon shows that "his mind is still chaos, and that he is not fit to be trusted with men's lives".*

THE LAST BATTLES

At the beginning of 1918, the trenches still snaked across the shattered land of northern France and Belgium as they had done at the end of 1914. But by 1918, things were changing.

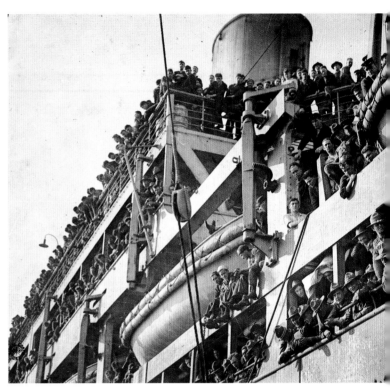

▲ *Hundreds of American soldiers fill the decks of a ship on their way to fight in Europe.*

Russia's new communist rulers had agreed a peace treaty with Germany in March 1918. Germany was able to concentrate all its efforts on the Western Front. However, the advantage would be short-lived as the first American troops started to arrive in France. Eventually the tide of troops and resources from across the Atlantic would surely overwhelm the Central Powers.

Ludendorff's offensive

By 21 March, the German commander Erich von Ludendorff launched his attack. His forces outnumbered the Allies, but he had little in reserve if reinforcements were needed. The first attack was launched against the British in the Somme area on 21 March 1918, using new techniques learned on the Eastern Front. The offensive was a success and by the end of May German forces were threatening Paris.

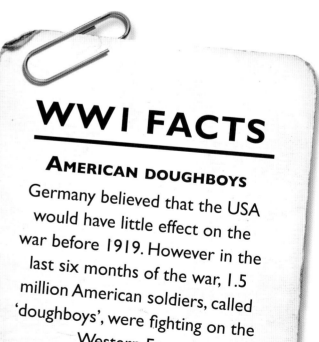

WWI FACTS

AMERICAN DOUGHBOYS

Germany believed that the USA would have little effect on the war before 1919. However in the last six months of the war, 1.5 million American soldiers, called 'doughboys', were fighting on the Western Front.

◀ In 1918, tanks helped to end the stalemate of trench warfare.

Fighting back

Although Germany continued to force the Allies back in July 1918, their position was weaker as the Allies, boosted by American troops, fought back over a wide area. Allied forces were backed by the supply of munitions, tanks, and aircraft from Britain and America, which could not be matched by war-weary Germany. In October, the Allies who had advanced along the whole Western Front, finally broke through the Hindenburg Line, Germany's last line of defence.

NATIONAL SERVICE
WOMEN CLERKS
WANTED AT ONCE

FOR
SERVICE IN FRANCE
WITH THE BRITISH ARMY

For Conditions of Service and Application Forms
APPLY
WOMEN'S SECTION NATIONAL

▲ American troops operating a field radio station. Radio communication on the battlefield was still difficult and complex in 1918.

▲ By 1918, troops on the Western Front were supported by thousands of female volunteers.

ARMISTICE

The fighting in World War I, or the Great War as it was called at the time, came to an end at 11.00 a.m. on 11 November 1918. In London, Paris and elsewhere, the news led to great celebrations.

▲ *A US sailor, French soldier and a Red Cross worker celebrate the Armistice in Paris.*

Everywhere, the end of the most destructive conflict in history was greeted with relief, like waking from a nightmare. For weeks before the armistice, the outcome of the war had not been in doubt. Germany was retreating on the Western Front, while her allies, Austria-Hungary, Turkey and Bulgaria had all collapsed. The Allies wanted to be certain that Germany could not restart the war. The Armistice was agreed early on 11 November but the fighting did not stop until 11 a.m. Tragically, around 10,000 soldiers were killed or wounded on that last morning of the war.

WW1 FACTS

TERMS OF THE ARMISTICE

The Armistice was signed on 11 November 1918. The Allies wanted to make sure that Germany could not restart the war. Germany was ordered to hand over 5000 heavy and field guns, 25,000 machine guns, 3000 trench mortars and 1700 aeroplanes. Germany also had to withdraw all troops from occupied areas within 15 days.

▲ *The German Fleet was taken to the British Royal Navy's base at Scapa Flow in the Orkney Isalnds. In June 1919, German sailors sunk most of the fleet to prevent them falling into Allied hands.*

Turmoil in Europe

The guns had fallen silent but things did not return to normal quickly. Germany was plunged into revolution as Kaiser Wilhelm II was forced to abdicate. Russians were already caught up in a brutal civil war. The blockade of Germany and Austria-Hungary continued until a peace treaty could be agreed, meaning that their people faced months of hunger.

by

. Lt. Siegfried Sassoon,

i Batt: Royal Welsh Fusiliers,

ly, 1917.

I am making this statement as an act of wilful defiance of
ilitary authority because I believe that the war is being deliberately
rolonged by those who have the power to end it. I am a soldier, con-
inced that I am acting on behalf of soldiers. I believe that the war
pon which I entered as a war of defence and liberation has now become
war of aggression and conquest. I believe that the purposes for which
and my fellow soldiers entered upon this war should have been so
learly stated as to have made it impossible to change them and that had
his been done the objects which actuated us would now be attainable by
egotiation.

I have seen and endured the sufferings of the troops and I
an no longer be a party to prolong these sufferings for ends which I
elieve to be evil and unjust. I am not protesting against the conduct
of the war, but against the political errors and insincerities for which
the fighting men are being sacrificed.

On behalf of those who are suffering now, I make this protest
against the deception which is being practised upon them; also I believe
it may help to destroy the callous complacency with which the majority
of those at home regard the continuance of agonies which they do not
share and which they have not enough imagination to realise.

WWI FACTS

LAST STAND IN AFRICA

General Paul von Lettow-Vorbeck was the last German commander to admit defeat. He finally surrendered in German East Africa when news of the Armistice reached him on 25 November 1918.

▲ German Kaiser Wilhelm II (centre) consults with his generals Paul von Hindenburg and Erich von Ludendorff.

▲ Siegfried Sassoon was one of many who felt that the war should have ended much sooner. In 1917 he wrote this statement, which was published in the British newspaper, The Times, saying that the "war of defence and liberation" had become a "war of aggression and conquest". In 1917, these views expressed by a war hero caused a scandal.

▼ Some of the hundreds of thousands of prisoners of war who had to be returned to their home countries at the end of the war.

▲ *After the war women in many countries were allowed to vote in elections for the first time.*

COST OF WAR

The cost of the war is almost impossible to calculate. Governments on both sides probably spent around $200 billion, but the true cost was far greater. When the peace treaty to end the war was finally agreed on 28 June 1919, Germany was forced by the victorious Allies to take the blame for starting the war and to pay for much of the damage done.

Millions of people died in World War I. Germany, France, Russia and Austria-Hungary all suffered more than a million deaths, while the British Empire lost at least 900,000 men. Millions more were so wounded or mentally damaged by the war that life was never the same again. Some victims of shell shock were never able to return to normal life. The figures for deaths during the war do not include at least 750,000 civilians who starved in central Europe or more than one million Armenians massacred in the Ottoman Empire during the war.

▶ *The Allied war leaders at the Paris Peace Conference: (Left to right) Britain's David Lloyd George, Italian Vittorio Orlando, Georges Clemenceau of France and US President Woodrow Wilson.*

▲ *Wounded soldiers in London celebrate the signing of the Treaty of Versailles.*

WW1 FACTS

SPANISH FLU

Immediately after the war, the world was hit by an epidemic of Spanish flu, which was spread by troops returning home. The illness claimed more lives than the war itself.

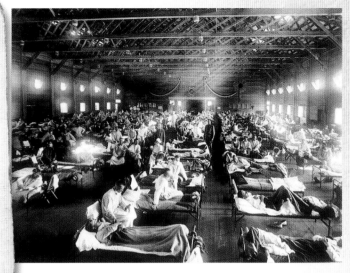

▲ *Victims of Spanish flu being treated in a temporary hospital.*

The old world crumbles

The war changed the world forever. The empires of Russia, Austria-Hungary and Ottoman Turkey collapsed. This created new or reborn countries such as Poland, but also led to new conflicts, including a terrible civil war in Russia. The Great Powers of the 1800s, including the vast British Empire, were fatally damaged by the cost of war. They were soon overtaken by the industrial might of the USA.

▶ *The German people were humiliated by the peace treaty that they were forced to accept by the Allies. Adolf Hitler (seated on the right) was able to exploit this bitterness in the 1930s as he unleashed World War II.*

LEST WE FORGET

The war touched families and communities across the world. Those who had gone off to fight failed to return home, or were changed forever by what they had experienced. Countries and communities found ways to remember those who had served in the war and many of these memorials survive today.

◀ *Most towns and villages in Britain, and many in other countries, are home to some kind of war memorial. These were set up by communities after the war. They were usually paid for by public subscription and listed the names of all those from the community or organisation who had died in the war. War memorials are the focus of ceremonies to remember the dead of World War I and other wars in November every year.*

▶ *Poppies were some of the first flowers to grow on the battlefields of the Western Front after the war. American Moina Michaels started selling poppies to raise money for war veterans. The idea spread to Europe, where Frenchwoman Anna Guerin presented a poppy to Field Marshall Haig, who supported the idea of the poppy as a symbol of remembrance.*

◄ In the fields once torn apart by the shells and gunfire of the Western Front, stand graves and memorials to those who died in the fighting there. Each British Empire soldier's death is marked with a headstone bearing their name. Almost half the bodies of those who died could not be identified. The headstones simply read: 'A Soldier of the Great War Known Unto God'.

▲ The body of an unidentified soldier is carried through London on 11 November 1920. The body was buried in the Tomb of the Unknown Warrior in Westminster Abbey, which commemorates the thousands of victims of the war whose bodies could not be identified.

◄ Second Lieutenant Eric Poole suffered shell shock after being caught up in a blast in the first week of the Battle of the Somme. After some time on leave, he went missing from his troops during a move to the frontline in October 1916. Despite his shell shock, Poole was found guilty of desertion at a court martial. This document is the statement Poole made in an attmpt to explain his actions were caused by his shell shock. He was the first British officer to be executed for cowardice on 10 December 1916. In 2006, the British government agreed to pardon more than 300 soldiers including Poole who were shot for cowardice.

World War I timeline

1914

28 June Assassination of Austrian Archduke Franz Ferdinand in Sarajevo, Bosnia by Serbian nationalist Gavrilo Princip, starting the chain of events that led to the outbreak of war.

28 July Austria-Hungary declares war on Serbia. By 4 August, Austria-Hungary and Germany are at war against Serbia, Russia, Belgium, France and Great Britain.

7 August British Secretary for War Lord Kitchener calls for 100,000 volunteers to form his New Army.

23 August British Expeditionary Force is forced to retreat by German forces at the Battle of Mons.

30 August Germany inflicts major defeat on invading Russian armies at Battle of Tannenberg.

6 September First Battle of the Marne ends German advance into France.

19 October Start of the First Battle of Ypres. The battle raged until 22 November, when the start of winter brought an end to the fighting.

29 October Ottoman Empire joins the war on the side of Germany and Austria.

November Trenches established for 750 kilometres along the Western Front from Switzerland to the North Sea.

16 December German warships bombard British coastal towns of Hartlepool, Whitby and Scarborough.

24 December Allied and German soldiers meet in no man's land in the Christmas Truce.

1915

22 April Poison gas is used for the first time by Germany at the start of the Second Battle of Ypres. This terrible weapon was later released by all sides.

25 April 70,000 troops from the British Empire and France land at Gallipoli in the Dardanelles. After heavy casualties, the last Allied troops were evacuated in January 1916.

7 May RMS Lusitania is sunk by a German submarine with the loss of around 1200 lives.

23 May Italy declares war on Austria-Hungary.

31 May Zeppelins attack London for the first time.

9 June British government creates the Ministry of Munitions to organize the supply of weapons after a 'shell crisis' that threatened the war effort.

25 September Major, but unsuccessful, Allied attack launched at Loos, including first use of poison gas by British troops.

6 October Serbia is invaded by Central Powers, including forces from Bulgaria. The remains of the Serbian army flees across the mountains of Albania.

5 December Turkish siege of Allied forces at Kut begins. Allied forces finally surrendered on 29 April 1916.

19 December Sir Douglas Haig succeeds Sir John French as Commander-in-Chief of British forces on the Western Front.

1916

9 February Britain introduces conscription for unmarried men, forcing them to join the armed forces.

21 February Battle of Verdun begins. More than a million men are killed and injured during ten months of fighting.

24 April Easter Rising by Irish nationalists in Dublin against British rule.

31 May The Battle of Jutland begins in the North Sea, forcing the German High Seas Fleet back to port for the rest of the war.

4 June Russian army begins the successful Brusilov Offensive against Austria-Hungary.

7 June The Arab Revolt begins against Turkish rule, supported by British officer T. E. Lawrence.

1 July First day of the Battle of the Somme, with 57,000 British troops killed or wounded in a single day.

15 September Tanks used for the first time during Battle of the Somme.

19 November Battle of the Somme ends. In almost five months, both sides suffer more than 600,000 casualties.

1 December Women's Army Auxiliary Corps set up in Britain, enabling women to fill supporting roles for the army.

1917

1 February Germany launches unrestricted submarine warfare, meaning that they will sink ships supplying the Allies without warning

8 March 'February Revolution' begins in Russia, forcing Tsar Nicholas II from power. Turmoil spreads to Russian forces, allowing Germany to move more troops to the Western Front.

26 March Allied advance into Palestine begins.

6 April USA declares war on Germany.

16 April French General Nivelle launches a disastrous offensive on the Chemin des Dames, leading to mutinies in the French army.

25 May Gotha heavy bombers attack Britain for the first time.

7 June British forces capture Messines Ridge following massive mine explosion that kills 10,000 German troops.

31 July Third Battle of Ypres, also known as Battle of Passchendaele, begins. The battle continues until November in horrific, muddy conditions with heavy casualties.

24 October Battle of Caporetto begins in northern Italy. The battle is a disaster for Italian forces with 275,000 soldiers taken prisoner and much of their artillery captured.

20 November Battle of Cambrai begins, with Allied forces using tanks and aircraft.

9 December Allied forces capture Jerusalem.

1918

3 March Russia's new Bolshevik government agrees peace with Germany at Treaty of Brest-Litovsk.

21 March Germany launches major attack on Western Front, forcing Allied forces to retreat.

15 July Second Battle of the Marne halts the German spring offensive.

8 August German lines are broken at the Battle of Amiens.

15 September Allied forces launch offensive from Salonika, Greece.

30 September British and Arab forces capture Damascus, the last major battle of the Middle-Eastern campaign.

30 October Turkey and Bulgaria agree to stop fighting. Austria-Hungary agrees an armistice on 3 November, leaving Germany alone against the Allies.

11 November Germany signs armistice with the Allies to end the war at 11 o'clock on the 11th day of the 11th month. Around 10,000 soldiers were killed and wounded on the last morning of the war.

25 November Last German forces, led by General Paul von Lettow-Vorbeck surrender in East Africa.

Aftermath

28 June 1919 Germany and the Allies sign the Treaty of Versailles, officially ending the war. Further treaties are later agreed with Germany's Allies.

11 November 1920 The Cenotaph war memorial is unveiled. Ceremonial burial of the Unknown Warrior in Westminster Abbey, London.

GLOSSARY

Allies countries fighting against the Central Powers, including Great Britain, France, Belgium, Russia and, later in the war, Italy and the USA

antibiotics medicines that can kill bacteria, the cause of infections and illness

ANZAC short for Australia and New Zealand Army Corps and describing troops from those countries who fought on the Allied side during World War I

armistice agreement to end fighting in a war

artillery heavy guns and cannons used to bombard enemy forces, usually moved around on wheels

blockade attempt to stop food and other supplies reaching a place by stopping or attacking ships or other vehicles

casualty soldier killed or wounded in battle

Central Powers Germany, Austria-Hungary and their allies during World War I

colony land that is ruled from overseas, such as the colonies that made up the British Empire in 1914

conscientious objector someone who refuses to fight in a war for religious, moral or other reasons

conscript someone who is not normally a soldier but is called into the armed forces during a war

conscription making it compulsory for people to join the armed forces, usually all able-bodied men between certain ages

court martial military court that judges actions of members of the armed forces, including refusal to follow orders

Defence of the Realm Act emergency laws passed in Britain that gave the government extra powers over industry and people during wartime

desertion leaving a military unit or post without permission

dominion self-governing parts of the British Empire, including Canada,

Australia, New Zealand and South Africa in 1914

Eastern Front border between the territory held by the Central Powers and Allies in Eastern Europe, where the two sides fought over territory

evacuate force people to leave somewhere to keep them safe

munitions material used in war, such as guns, shells, and other ammunition

nation country or community made up of people with a common language or culture

nationalist someone who has strong views or uses force on behalf of their country or people, for example when campaigning for independence from another country

no man's land strip of land between two opposing lines of trenches or fortifications, where fighting takes place

Ottoman Empire empire ruled from Constantinople in Turkey that included large parts of the Middle East, North Africa, and south-eastern Europe before World War I

propaganda information designed to promote a particular point of view, usually that of the government

rationing restriction of food and other items to ensure that there is enough to go round

reconnaissance gathering information about enemy forces and tactics

reinforcements extra forces arriving to help in a battle and replace those killed or wounded

shell explosive fired from a piece of artillery or cannon

ultimatum demand which has to be met within a set period of time to avoid consequences, such as military action

Western Front border between the territory held by the Central Powers and the Allies in France and Belgium, where the two sides fought over territory

FIND OUT MORE
Books

See Inside the First World War by Rob Lloyd Jones and Maria Cristina Pritelli (Usborne, 2013)

Women in World War I by Nick Hunter (Raintree, 2013)
Discover more about the lives of women around the world during wartime.

Brothers at War: A First World War Family History by Sarah Ridley (Franklin Watts, 2013) Using letters, diaries and other documents, this book tells the story of a family's experiences during World War I.

Forgotten Voices of the Great War by Max Arthur (Ebury / Imperial War Museum, 2003) A fascinating book packed with eyewitness accounts by those who fought in and lived through the war

Men, Women and Children in the First World War by Philip Steele (Wayland, 2013)

My Brother's Keeper by Tom and Tony Bradman (A&C Black, 2014)

Online resources

The National Archives have created a fantastic online resource covering many aspects of World War I
www.nationalarchives.gov.uk/education/greatwar/

The Imperial War Museum is home to a vast collection of artefacts and resources from World War I. It's well worth a visit but you can also discover lots through the museum's website at **www.iwm.org.uk**

There are many other museums that tell the story of the war. Your local museum may explain how your home town was changed by the war. Other museums tell the story of certain aspects of the conflict, such as the National Army Museum. Find out more at **www.nam.ac.uk**

You can also find out more about other countries and how they remember the war. The Australian National War memorial website is a great place to find out about the ANZACs' role in the conflict. **www.awm.gov.au/atwar/ww1.asp**

A The National Archives

The National Archives is the UK government's official archive containing over 1,000 years of history. They give detailed guidance to government departments and the public sector on information management, and advise others about the care of historical archives.

www.nationalarchives.gov.uk

The National Archives picture acknowledgements and catalogue references

P4 WO95-820 (1) Somme War Diary Entry, 1916. P 7 WO 71/1236 (1914) Trial of German spy Carl Hans Lody. P 8 CAB 20/4 Schlieffen Plan map. P10 P11 NATS1-109 National Service Poster. P15 RAIL253-516 (1) Christmas card from the Front. P17 EXT1-315 1 of 2 German trenches before bombardment (2 images). P18 RAIL253-516 2 of 2 Postcard message from Jack Symons 27 September 1915. P18-19 RAIL253-516 Postcard 1 of 2 from Pte H Giles November 1915. P19 RAIL253-516 Hut accommodation at the Front 1915-1918. P23 PRO 30/57/61. P27 WO95-1653 (1) War Diary 20 Infantry Brigade 1916. P29 WO339-51440 Siegfried Sassoon Medical board proceedings 1917. P30 NSC7-37 Food Control Campaign Adopt Voluntary Rations 1916-1917. P31 HO 45/10734/258927 Telegram on licensing hours changes during wartime. P32 AIR 1/569/16/15/142. P32 MEP0 2/1621. P35 MAF42-8 Womens' Land Army armlet 1917-1918. P35 MAF59-3 Womens' Land Army girls with piglets. P35 NATS1-109 War Work Enrol Today Release A Fit Man For the Front 1914-1918. P35 NATS1-109 WAAC Releases A Man for the BEF 1914-1918. P36 EXT1-315 Pt2 Women Come And Help poster WWI. P37 MUN5-289 National Projectile Factory Hackney Marshes Boring 6 Shells 1916. P37 EXT1-315 Rules for the use of trinitrotoluene 1917. P39 EXT1-315 Pt10 (2) No Holidays. P41 HO45/10808/31118. P43 ADM137-3923. P43 ADM 1/8331. P44-45 WO 95/2756. P46 MUN 5/394. P49 WO138-74 Lieut Wilfred E S Owen killed in action 1918. P49 WO339-51440 Siegfried Sassoon concern over state of mental health 1918. P51 NATS 1/109 (2). P53 WO339-51440 Siegfried Sassoon's document accusing authorities of prolonging the war 1918. P53 FO383-413 (4) French and British POWs arrive at camp from the front, World War I, 1918. P54 EXT1-315 Learn EXT1-315 Learn To Make Munitions poster. P57 WO 71/1027 (c. 24 Nov 1916; 3 Dec 1916; 10 Dec 1916).

PICTURE ACKNOWLEDGEMENTS

1 MacDonald, Lyn, 1914-1918: Voices and Images of the Great War, Penguin, 1991. p156
2 Clark, Lloyd, World War I: An Illustrated History, p34
3 Arthur, Max, Forgotten Voices of the Great War, Ebury, 2002. p113
4 https://www.princeton.edu/~achaney/tmve/wiki100k/docs/World_War_I_casualties.html
5 http://www.nam.ac.uk/exhibitions/online-exhibitions/waacs-war
6 http://www.bbc.co.uk/news/mobile/magazine-17011607

INDEX